D1389297

OUTDOOR SCIENCE

PLANTS

Sonya Newland

WAYLAND
www.waylandbooks.co.uk

First published in Great Britain in 2018 by Wayland

Produced for Wayland by
White-Thomson Publishing Ltd
www.wtpub.co.uk

Editor: Sonya Newland
Design: Rocket Design (East Anglia) Ltd
Illustrations: TechType
Consultant: James Thomson

ISBN: 978 1 5263 0938 9
10 9 8 7 6 5 4 3 2 1

Wayland
An imprint of
Hachette Children's Group
Part of Hodder & Stoughton
Carmelite House
50 Victoria Embankment
London EC4Y 0DZ

An Hachette UK Company
www.hachette.co.uk
www.hachettechildrens.co.uk

Printed in China

Picture acknowledgements:
iStock: Instants 5tr, MarioGuti 5bl, chameleonseye 5br, ljubaphoto 7t, mikeuk 8m, BogWan 11, snapgalleria 14, amenic181 15t, paulbein 18t, Antagain 18ml, GlobalP 18mc, Liliboas 18mr, Antagain 18bl, AlexStar 18bc, DNY59 23ltl, 23rtl, Delpixart 23rm, Kerrick 23rr, Rachel_Web_Design 23b, kamisoka 24t, kickimages 24b, rperlstrom 25t; Shutterstock: RethaAretha 4t, Tine Snels 4b, alybaba 5tl, Teguh Mujiono 6, Filipe B. Varela 7b, IamOkay 7ml, Yellowj 7mr, Medtech THAI STUDIO LAB 249 8t, Dory F 8bl, olpo 8br, By P.S.Art-Design-Studio 9, Vladimir Konstantinov 10tl, adison pangchai 10tr, gresei 10ml, Nito 10mr, Joang Hongyan 10bl, Valentina Razumova 10br, Kazakova Maryia 10b, Eag1eEyes 12t, Radu Burcan 15b, Chad Zuber 16t, Allocricetulus 18br, Dredger 19t, Marian Piris 19b, lcrms 20t, Wolfgang Kruck 22l, struvictory 22r, Maksym Bondarchuk 23ltr, 23lbl, 23lbr, 23rbl, jessicahyde 25m, Robofly 25b, Peter Zijlstra 26t, Stone36 26bl, Andrii Zastrozhnov 26br, vvoe 27tl, Garsya 27tc, Madlen 27tr, audaxl 27ml, LedyX 27mr, MNStudio 27b, photogal 28t.

Illustrations on pages 12, 13, 16, 17, 20 and 21 by TechType.

All design elements from Shutterstock.

Contents

What are plants?

If you look outside, you'll see plants everywhere. They come in all shapes, sizes and colours.

Plants for life

Plants are essential to life on Earth. They provide food and shelter for animals. They create the oxygen that people need to breathe. Without plants, neither humans nor animals could survive.

Plants are the only type of food that deer and other herbivores eat.

Air plants often wind their roots around other plants, such as trees.

Where do plants grow?

Most plants grow in soil. Some plants, such as algae, live in water. Others are 'air plants'. These amazing plants can grow above ground, without any soil.

Can you spot a ground plant, a water plant and an air plant outside?

Types of plants

There are many different types of plants.

Around 80 per cent of plants produce flowers. Roses, corn and strawberries are all flowering plants.

Non-flowering plants include ferns and mosses. Ferns are among the oldest plants in the world. They were around when dinosaurs roamed the Earth.

Trees are the tallest plants in the world. They are a type of woody plant. Some shrubs are also woody plants. Woody plants can also be flowering plants.

There are even some plants that eat meat! These carnivorous plants trap insects for food.

parts of a plant

Plants are made of several parts. Each part plays an important role in helping the plant grow and survive.

flower

leaf

fruit

stem

root

Flower

The flowers are the part of the plant that produces seeds. The seeds create new plants.

Leaf

The stem is linked to tiny veins in the leaves. Water and nutrients are carried into the leaf. There they mix with sunlight and carbon dioxide. This makes food for the plant.

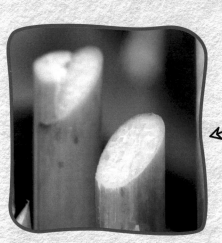

Stem

The straw-like stem is made up of lots of little tubes. It supports the part of the plant that is above ground. The stem holds the leaves and flowers up nearer the Sun. Water and nutrients travel from the roots up the stem.

Roots

The roots draw water and nutrients from the soil. The plant needs these things to live. Some water and nutrients are stored in the roots until the plant needs them. The roots spread out in the soil. They hold the plant securely in the ground.

Comparing plants

Can you identify different types of plant? Do you know the names of all their parts?

You will need:

✷ paper

✷ coloured pencils

✷ a tape measure or long ruler

bluebell (flowering plant)

Step 1

Find an area outside that has a good variety of plants. Choose three plants. Try to find:

✷ a flowering plant

✷ a non-flowering plant

✷ a woody plant

fern (non-flowering plant)

blackthorn shrubs (woody plant)

Step 2

Draw a picture of each plant. Label the different parts.

flower

leaf

stem

Step 3

Create a table to help you compare your plants. Give each plant a column. Then answer these questions for each one.

* How big is it?

* What shape is it?

* What colour is it?

* Does it have flowers?

* What does it smell like?

Step 4

Now see if you can answer these questions to discover if you are a plant expert!

* What type of plant is each one? How do you know?

* How are your plants the same and how are they different?

* Do you notice anything about the ways they are the same and the ways they are different? Does the biggest plant have the biggest stem? What about the leaves?

⚠ REMEMBER

* Always check with an adult before touching plants. Some of them are poisonous. Wash your hands carefully afterwards.

Super seeds

All living things have a life cycle. A plant's life cycle begins with a seed ...

poppy seeds

pumpkin seeds

cocoa beans

broad beans

avocado seed

coconut

Seed shapes and sizes

Seeds can be as small as a grain of sand, but some are much bigger. Conkers are seeds, for example. Edible seeds are sometimes called beans. Nuts may also be seeds. Seeds can be round, flat or shaped like a drop of water.

Structure of a seed

Inside a seed is a tiny plant. This is called the embryo. The seed's hard outer casing protects the embryo. Small leaves on the seed carry food to the embryo.

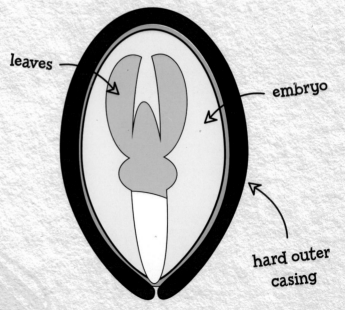

leaves

embryo

hard outer casing

Germination

Germination is the first stage of plant growth. Some seeds need light to germinate. Others need to be in the dark. Most seeds need moisture and oxygen. If the conditions are right, the embryo starts to grow. As it gets bigger, it breaks through the casing. Tiny leaves appear.

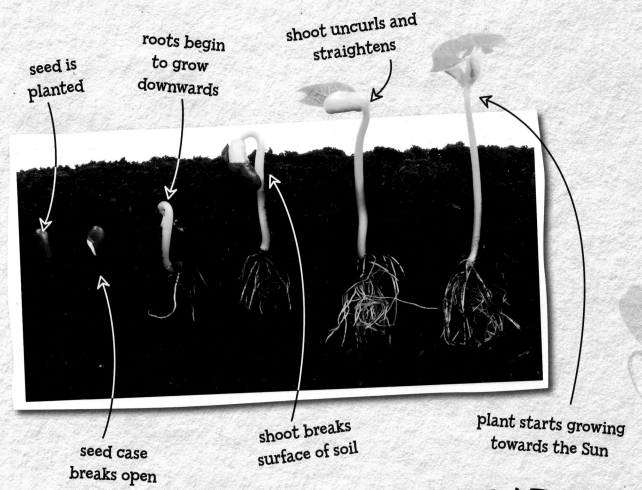

seed is planted

roots begin to grow downwards

shoot uncurls and straightens

seed case breaks open

shoot breaks surface of soil

plant starts growing towards the Sun

HANDS On!

Collect as many different types of seed as you can. Lay them out in order of size, from the smallest to the biggest. Measure each seed and write down how big it is. How big is your biggest seed? Do you know which plant it comes from?

SPOT IT!

Can you spot any new plants just pushing through the soil outside?

Going underground

Plant seeds in a glass jar. Then watch what happens below and above ground as they germinate and grow!

You will need:
* a glass jar
* kitchen roll
* water
* broad bean seeds

Step 1

Fill the jar with kitchen roll.

Step 2

Pour in enough water to make the kitchen roll wet, but not so much that water collects at the bottom. Add more damp kitchen towel until it is packed tightly.

Step 3

Push the bean seeds down the side of the jar, so you can see them clearly through the glass.

Step 4

Keep the jar outside in a place that is warm but out of direct sunlight. Check the jar every day. Add water to keep the kitchen roll damp if you need to.

Step 5

Watch the seeds grow! Keep a daily diary of your plant's progress.

WHY NOT TRY? Do the same experiment with different types of seed. Try a flower seed and a cucumber seed. How quickly do they germinate and grow? How does this compare to the bean seed?

Growing UP

Plants need three things to help them grow
- water, the Sun and carbon dioxide.

How do plants grow?

Plants need energy to grow. They get this through photosynthesis.

The leaves take in carbon dioxide from the air.

The carbon dioxide mixes with the water in the leaves.

It goes into the tiny veins in the leaves.

The water travels up through the stem.

With a little help from the Sun, this turns into oxygen and a sugar called glucose.

The roots draw up water from the soil.

Glucose gives the plant the energy it needs to grow.

Energy from the Sun

The Sun is a key ingredient in photosynthesis. Sunlight contains energy. This is absorbed by a special chemical in the leaves of the plant, called chlorophyll. Chlorophyll is green, which is why most plants are green.

The word 'photosynthesis' means 'putting together with light'.

Sugar for growth

Plants absorb sunlight in their leaves. At the same time, they take in water from their roots and carbon dioxide from the air. Together, these three things make glucose. Glucose is a sugar – and sugar is packed with energy! The plant uses the glucose as food to help it grow.

'Breathing' plants

Did you know that plants 'breathe'? This is called respiration. In respiration, the oxygen and glucose become carbon dioxide and water. These are 'breathed' out of the plant through tiny holes in the leaves. The holes are called stomata.

SPOT IT!

Look at the underside of a leaf through a magnifying glass. Can you spot the stomata?

stomata

'Crying' leaves

Plants release water as well as carbon dioxide. In fact, nearly all the water a plant takes in comes out through its leaves. See for yourself ...

In some countries, people collect fresh drinking water this way!

You will need:

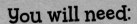

* a clear plastic bag such as a food freezer bag
* an elastic band
* a large leaf (still attached to the tree or plant!)

Step 1

Find a large leaf on a tree or plant.

Step 2

Cover the leaf with the plastic bag. Secure the bag with the elastic band.

Step 3

Watch for a couple of minutes. Does the bag start to mist up? What do you think is happening?

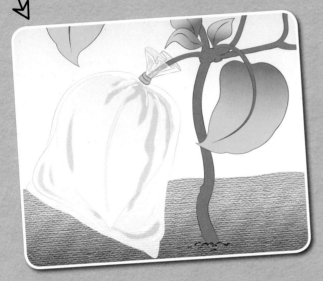

Step 4

Go back in an hour and see what has happened. Have droplets of water formed inside the bag? Why do you think this is?

WHY NOT TRY?

See how much water collects in the bag for eight hours during the day. Then leave the bag for eight hours overnight. Is there more or less water in the bag? Why do you think that is?

pollinating plants

Plants make more plants through pollination. This starts in the flower.

Pollen

Inside flowers, there is a dusty substance called pollen. When pollen from one flower lands on another, a seed forms. This is called pollination. The seed is the start of a new plant.

Insects are very important in making new plants. Pollinators are insects that spread pollen between flowers.

These insects are all pollinators.

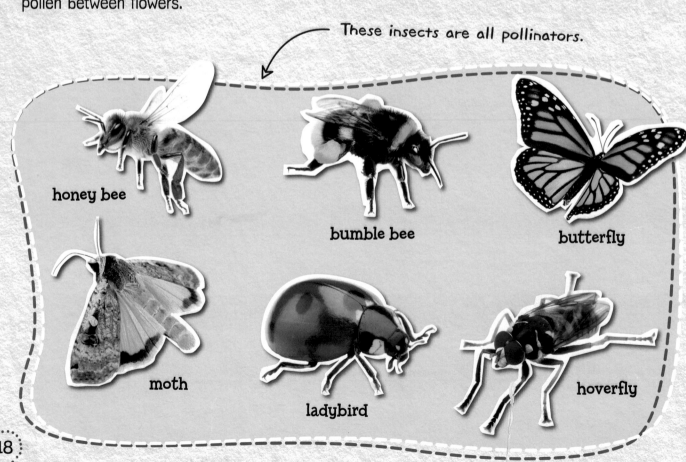

honey bee

bumble bee

butterfly

moth

ladybird

hoverfly

Nectar hunters

Pollinators such as bees are attracted to the bright colours and nice smell of flowers. They know this means that there is nectar in the flower. Nectar is a sugary liquid that bees love. They use it to make honey.

Pollinating power

Bees burrow in flowers to reach the nectar. As they burrow, pollen sticks to them. They carry the pollen with them to the next flower. Pollination begins and a new plant is created.

Bees get pollen on them when looking for nectar.

Carried on the wind

The wind is also a pollinator. Pollen is very light. When the wind blows, pollen can be carried between plants.

HANDS on!

Bees and other pollinators need water. Try making a 'bee bath'. Put pebbles in the bottom of a small dish. Fill the dish with water. Leave it somewhere outside for the bees to enjoy!

Build a bee hotel

Pollinators are very important to the environment. Encourage them to visit your local area by building a place for them to stay.

You will need:

* hollow bamboo canes
* a waterproof carton such as a plastic water bottle
* scissors
* string

Step 1

Cut the top off the carton or plastic bottle.

Step 2

Cut or break the bamboo canes so they are the same length as the main part of the bottle.

Step 3

Pack the canes tightly in the bottle. There should not be much room between them.

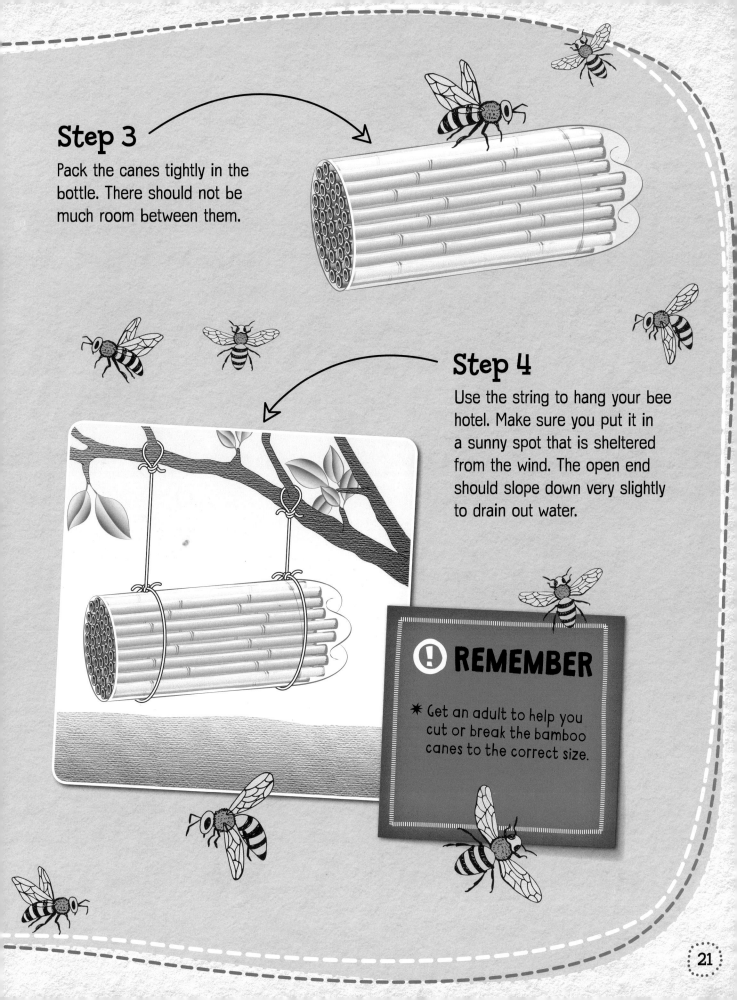

Step 4

Use the string to hang your bee hotel. Make sure you put it in a sunny spot that is sheltered from the wind. The open end should slope down very slightly to drain out water.

(!) REMEMBER

* Get an adult to help you cut or break the bamboo canes to the correct size.

All about trees

Trees are like other plants. They have roots, leaves and a stem (the trunk). They also come in many different shapes and sizes.

Types of tree

There are two main types of tree, deciduous and evergreen.

Deciduous trees lose their leaves. In countries where the temperatures get quite low, leaves fall in autumn. The trees are bare for the winter.

Evergreen trees do not lose their leaves. They keep them all year round. Evergreen trees usually have long, straight trunks. Their branches are also straight and even.

deciduous trees

evergreen trees

oak

ash

cherry

horse chestnut

pine

holly

cypress

sequoia

Pine cones

Not all trees have flowers. So, where are the seeds? In trees such as pine and cypress, they are in the cones. Cones are closed in wet weather. In dry weather, the cones open. The seeds are carried away on the wind.

HANDS on!

Go to a wooded area. Try to identify which are evergreen trees and which are deciduous trees.

How old is that tree?

The wider the trunk of a tree is, the older it usually is.

You will need:
* ✳ a tape measure
* ✳ a notebook
* ✳ a friend!

Step 1

Measure the trunk. Find a tree near your house or school. Measure how big the trunk is all the way round. How many inches is it? That number is roughly how many years old the tree is.

⊙ REMEMBER

✳ If you are measuring in centimetres, divide the trunk's size by 2.5. This will tell you how big it is in inches.

Step 2

Count the rings. Find the stump of a tree that has been chopped down. Carefully count the number of rings. Each ring marks one year of the tree's life. A wide ring means it was a rainy year. A narrow ring means a year where there was not much rain. How many rainy years can you count?

Compare the rings on two tree trunks. Do they show the same rainy years and sunny years?

(!) REMEMBER

* Start with the outer ring and work inwards. That way you will be comparing the same years.

Dark marks on the rings mean the tree was damaged in that year.

WHY NOT TRY?

Look around the base of a tree. What different parts can you collect? Search for leaves, cones, fruit, berries and bark. Can you find any other parts?

fruit and vegetables

Are fruit and vegetables plants?
Not exactly. They are *parts* of plants.

Fruit or veg?

The fruit is the part of a plant that contains the seeds. Vegetables are any other parts that you can eat.

You might think that a tomato is a vegetable. But look inside! A tomato is a fruit.

Raspberries and blackberries are made up of lots of tiny fruits. There is a seed inside each part.

Soft or hard?

Some fruits are soft on the outside. Peaches, plums and strawberries are all easy to bite into. But other fruits have a hard outer casing. Think about a melon or a mango. You have to slice through a hard outer casing to reach the juiciness inside.

watermelon

Underground ...

Some vegetables grow completely underground. To eat potatoes, carrots and beetroot, you have to dig them up first.

carrots

beetroot

potatoes

... or overground?

Other vegetables, such as lettuce, peppers and pumpkins, grow above ground.

lettuce

peppers

pumpkins

SPOT IT!

How many types of wild fruit can you spot? Do not eat the fruit!

Create your own garden

Create a container garden to grow your own fruit and vegetables.

You will need:

* three containers (old buckets or bags for growing plants)
* seeds (cherry tomatoes, carrots, strawberries or any other fruit or veg you like)
* soil
* a trowel

Step 1

Put your containers in a sunny but sheltered spot.

Step 2

Fill them with soil.

Step 3

Dig small holes in the soil with the trowel. Follow the instructions on the seed packets. These will tell you how deep the holes should be, and how far apart.

Step 4

Decide what to grow in each container. Then carefully place a seed in each hole.

Step 5

Water your container garden every day. Check to see how your fruit and vegetables are coming along!

⊙ REMEMBER

* Do not eat the fruit straight away. Always wash it first. Make sure an adult has said it's safe to eat.

Glossary

algae – a type of plant that lives in water

carbon dioxide – a gas present in the air

carnivorous – something that eats meat

edible – things that can be eaten

embryo – the first stage of a new living thing

germination – the process by which plants begin to grow

glucose – a type of sugar made in plants, which they use for energy

nectar – a sugary liquid made in plants to attract pollinators

nutrients – substances that living things need to grow and survive

oxygen – a gas present in the air

photosynthesis – the process by which plants get energy and make food

poisonous – something that can make you ill

pollen – the dusty substance inside flowers that helps make new plants

pollinator – an insect that helps plants pollinate

respiration – the process in which plants release carbon dioxide and water

stomata – tiny holes on the underside of leaves

further reading

Books

The Amazing Life Cycle of Plants (Look and Wonder)
by Kay Barnham and Maddie Frost (Wayland, 2018)

Plants (Moving up with Science)
by Peter Riley (Franklin Watts, 2016)

Plants (Amazing Science)
by Sally Hewitt (Wayland, 2014)

Websites

Find out all about plants with this interactive website
www.dkfindout.com/uk/animals-and-nature/plants/

Use this page as a starting point for exploring all sorts of plant facts, with games, quizzes and pictures
www.sciencekids.co.nz/plants.html

Visit this page for an assortment of plant facts
www.scienceforkidsclub.com/plants.html

Index

OUTDOOR SCIENCE

Titles in the series

MATERIALS

What are materials?

Wonderful wood

Build a lolly stick raft

Mighty metal

Rugged rock

Make a sedimentary rock

Super soil

Separate soil

Man-made materials

Test waterproof materials

Solids, liquids and gases

Changing state

Make an ice sculpture

PLANTS

What are plants?

Parts of a plant

Comparing plants

Super seeds

Going underground

Growing up

'Crying' leaves

Pollinating plants

Build a bee hotel

All about trees

How old is that tree?

Fruit and vegetables

Create your own garden

ANIMALS

Animals everywhere

Types of animals

Make a paint trap

Animals in the earth

Bug hunting

Awesome insects

Plant a butterfly habitat

Hard-to-spot animals

Nocturnal animal spotting

Amazing amphibians

Tracking tadpoles

In the air

Name that song

HABITATS

What are habitats?

What lives where?

Animal identification

Food chains

Habitat hunting

What's in the pond?

Make a mini-pond

Log life

Minibeast hunt

Rock pools

Name that shell!

In the grass

Be a habitat hero

WEATHER

What is weather?

Windy weather

Make an anemometer

Sunshine and shadows

Measuring shadows

Clouds and rain

Evaporation in action

Snow and ice

Melting ice

Thunder and lightning

Make a rain gauge

Wild weather

Make a wind catcher

FORCES

What are forces?

Measuring forces

Playground forces

Forces and motion

Make a bottle rocket

Attractive gravity

Spin the bucket

Surface friction

Testing surfaces

Air and water resistance

Make an egg parachute

Amazing magnetism

Make a compass